A Playbook on Life for Young Athletes

By Nate McGhee & Contributing Authors

dom·i·nate

ˈdäməˌnāt/

Have a commanding influence on, exercise control, be the most important or conspicuous person or thing in.
(Syn. Assertive, Powerful, leading, effective, influential, Prevailing, Ascendant)

Dedicated to my nephew Amir Gregory Benson, and all the boys destined to one day be MENtors to the game of life!

All rights reserved. Dominate Copyrighted 2018

Hey Brotha,
My name is Nathaniel Parker McGhee, from Saint Louis, MO (STL). I am an Athletic Scholar with dreams to be a successful businessman in the NFL. All my life I have had my dad, grandfathers, coaches and mentors that have given me a template for life! I would like to call it a playbook. I reached out to ask a few good MEN (**Men**tors) to write you letters, poems or drop a piece of advice that you can add to your personal playbook, so get ready to take notes.

Growing up in the STL, also known as the Show-Me-State has taught me that your words need to be followed up with your actions.

My high school, Chaminade College Preparatory, prepared me for life with the motto "Esto Vir" to be a MAN!
Just know being a man means you will make mistakes, more than once but you should try not repeat them and be responsible for your actions. You must hold yourself accountable.

As long as I can remember as a football player and student of the game of life I have had different **Men**tors from all walks of life to drop knowledge, give me advice, teach me to have confidence and the courage to make informed choices in life. It was a gift to me, that I felt should be shared with you! I saw them all as plays that you must read, study, and practice.

Most importantly, I learned how to be a man! How to lose, win, fall, get back up and start over again. How to be mentally strong, respect yourself and know life is definitely about YOU defining your own path and not allowing society to define you!

My dad has always been in my life and he taught me to always respect myself, speak the truth and be humble. As a lover of the game, he instills stories of wisdom over, and over again. I sat there, listened and took mental notes. My mom taught me to keep GOD & family first! As well as to always be humble, speak my mind and to be a peacekeeper. My parents instilled in me from birth that I was born a leader, and that in our family McGhee's make it happen. I was born on New Year's Eve, I came six weeks early, I was always fast. I was actually supposed to be due on Super bowl Sunday.

My family had already nicknamed me (TD) the touchdown baby. I guess I had my mind made up when I came early. The doctor still nicknamed me (TD) said, I was a tax deduction, haha. See, told you I was born a natural leader, knowing my worth! I came into the world making money. LOL.

I was also my parents' only son, with two older sisters who empowered me to know we all have our own path. They have my back and front, but we all know who was running it! Always trying to keep me in check, but I learned the game from them and dominated it! I hope as you read Dominate, you too will begin to explore what it means to define your journey as well! In football, I have played many positions, today I'm a cornerback. No matter what sport you play, the most important will be the game of life. Growing up in my Ferguson/Florissant community I personally experienced my community fall apart in August of 2014 due to the killing of Mike Brown, the protest, and the importance of the rise of young black **men**tors like myself who needed to know that my life matters.

Please note, all young men need to know they have a voice, a purpose strong **men**tors, role models and community that will support you. I feel all these **men**tors empowered me to define my path. Now it is your time.

Wait…Guess what? I'm not done yet; I'm still growing, but I also know we are never too old to learn; so let's' get it! Use these tools to dominate life. This book leaves space for you to take notes, journal and practice the plays that will guide you to define your identity as a MAN! Enjoy your journey, know that even if you don't have a family you always have God, as it says in the bible Romans 5:8, I loved you at your darkest. Remember, God will always have your back! Stay in touch!

Your BrothaKeeper, **Men**tor & Friend,
Nate Parker McGhee
#DomiNateSTL

Table of Contents

D.O.M.I.N.A.T.E   8
Let's GO.   10
G.R.I.T.   12
R.E.A.L Man.   16
Man CHILD.   20
A Walk in My Shoes   22
The Brush.   31
The Main Event.   36
The Men Tour   40
The Game.   43
T.T.G   47
Define your Dreams   51
Nate's Playbook-Sayins.   56
Nate's Favorite Quotes.   59
What does Dominate mean?   62

D.O.M.I.N.A.T.E

D-Determination! Do you! Know that society doesn't define you, know that every goal starts with a beginning and you must never give up until you reach the end

O-Optimistic Own your mistakes, learn from them

M-Motivation- Motivation Move Forward

I-Intellect Inspire yourself with understanding

N-Navigate Never give up on your destiny

A-Articulate Affirm your assets with your words

T-Trust Teach brothers to respect one another

E-Educate Empower yourself

*Men*tal *Note:*
Define what "Dominate" means to you or create your own acronym?

Let's GO!

It's time to **Dominate**.
Get your head in a space that allows you to take flight! The sky's the limit, but you must be **Determined** to fly when the time comes to take flight.

How **Optimistic** are you to win it? Who and what will stop you? I hope the answer is nothing or no one! Because you need to be in control of your tomorrow!

Now, think about what is your **Motivation?** What is it your individual struggles or your collective responsibility to yourself and your family? What mark will you leave on society? Be motivated to be a leader! It's time to leave a legacy! You need to use your mind to seek knowledge & your voice to deliver solutions!

Whether you're a scholar-athlete, learning a trade, or an entrepreneur your **Intellect** needs to be a part of your business plan! Being mentally, physically, emotionally, spiritually & financially stable will make you an asset! If you are not an asset, then you're a debit which means you don't value your networth!

Know how to **Navigate** your map to success! In order to be a success you need to know self-worth, you need to know education is key and knowledge doesn't always come from a book, but you must surround yourself around a circle that doesn't place you in a box. How do you **Articulate** your needs and wants? Be straightforward and honest. Use your voice and know your word is bond. Remember to **Trust** your gut; but know that trust and faith go hand in hand, you must have confidence in yourself and belief from within.

This is the difference between what makes a boy a man! Being **Educated** is a lifetime commitment so commit! Sign on the dotted line. Create the contract you want to live by and then dominate it! Time to define your hour, your time, your place in history! Let's Go! It's time to **Dominate!**

Mental Note:

Define what your game plan will be. Create your Contract. List three goals you want to meet this year? Ready, Set, Let's GO…

Sign (your name here)

_____

G.R.I.T

Dear Young Man,

You are growing up in a world today were you need to be ready for a great journey that will have known, unknowns and fatal unknowns. Be ready to learn, challenge yourself at every step, and be ready to get back up at every fall.

Have GRIT...as every great story happened when someone decided not to give up.
Grit is sticking with your future day in, day out and not just for the week, not just for the month, but for years.
Every day do something that will inch you closer to a better tomorrow and have the courage to follow your heart and intuition. They somehow already know what you truly want to become.

Lastly, VOLUNTEER!!!! I have made more friends, developed more relationships, and have grown the most when I was trying to HELP OTHERS versus using them for my benefit...You will get back tenfold what you give into it...trust me!

A defining moment in my life was when I had to decide whether to leave my home, comfort and the known of St Louis, and venture out to college in Alabama on a football scholarship at Tuskegee University to a city, place and culture that I had never been; to a place where I had zero friends, no family just a packed bag and the will to seek out and understand.

This experience grew me mentally, spiritually, and educationally, as I had to learn how to spread $20 over two weeks at a time, walk to everything I needed, make new friends and learn new things.

This experience cultivated my ability to fail fast, fail often and fail forward realizing that it was the journey and what I learned along the way, and how it grew me that was the purpose of doing it anyway. You see in the black community we are AFRAID to take risks and explore. You must make sure you travel to as many places that you can, explore how other people and cultures live. *I promise it will be an invaluable experience!*

Today, I am a Vice President of a major 15 Billion dollar company here in Charlotte, NC where I moved in June of 2018 another great adventure I have set upon with my family so that we can grow and mature and learn once again. So, we can fail fast, fail often and fail forward and learn together.

I aspire to become a Business Unit President; where I will preside over 12,000+ People, and a large segment of the business to drive success so that as a Black man, I may open doors, create opportunities, and mentor young men like me to stretch beyond what I have been able to achieve myself.

To pass on my successes,
my grit and determination to my daughters, so that they can build and grow past my own personal achievements.

If I were to sum up my journey with a quote, I would say,
" *Be ready to fail, and embrace failure, have grit and determination to persevere as its difference between the impossible and the possible lies in a man's determination...as real man smiles at trouble, gathers strength from distress, and grows brave by reflection and applies it to succeed*"

Sincerely,
Cory J Sauls, CSSBB, CPIM, PMP
Coach, Mentor

Mental Note:

Define what G.R.I.T means to you?

R.E.A.L MAN

Dear Young Man,
I speak with you from a place, in which you have been instrumental along my journey. I speak with you from a place of accumulated knowledge, lessons learned, and stories told that ring with the echoes of wisdom. One of the many lessons that I share with you is that knowledge is information obtained, while wisdom is knowledge applied. I implore you to believe in the greatness that you are, the greatness that you shall be, and the greatness in others that you shall inspire.

As a mentor, the assumption is that we are the teachers and/or leaders of others, yet this is only partial truth. You have empowered me to be a better listener, so that when I speak you shall find value in the knowledge that I impart upon you. Thank you for trusting me with your thoughts.

As our brotherhood evolves and trust is established we then discuss manhood and what it means to be a R.E.A.L. Man.

Together we will discuss and define **R**espect, breaking it down into two parts; respectability and respectfulness. We will engage in conversations on **E**ducation, agreeing that education Is achieved in the classroom as well as on the streets.

Wanting the best for each other we had a dialogue on **A**ccountability; and being humble enough so that we may keep each other focused on our goals.

As I stood before you, we entertained the ideology of **L**eadership, understanding that as I stand before you, one day you will stand before my son, and as the cycle goes on, my son will stand before yours.

Your leadership impacts more than your today or your tomorrow – your leadership shall be the driving force towards the success for future generations.

Young Man, you are a R.E.A.L Man by every sense of the phrase… Stand Tall, Stand Strong, Stand with Confidence with your shoulders back, chest out, head up and with your eyes exposed to the light!
I believe in you, I love you, and I look forward to celebrating your GREATNESS!

Your Brother, Rennell Parker, Sr.
Father, Mentor, Author, Life Consultant,
Founder of The Parker Group
United States Navy Veteran

*Men*tal *Note:*

Define what being a **R.E.A.L** Man means to you?

Man-child

Man-child you hold our future in your hands
Man-child learn from Men & Women who walk on a straight path!
Man-child learn from men and women that walked on a crooked path!
Man-child strives for perfection in everything you do.
Man-child Love with all your might
Man-child never take time for granted
Man-child Love God with all your might
Man-child Love your family with all your might
Man-child always do what needs to be done
Man-child be a Man amongst men
This is what a Man-Child must do.

By AG

*Men*tal *Note:*

Man-Child what dreams or goals do you have for your life? Start with goals for the next month, next year, then explore next 4 years. Write out your dreams as well. You got this! Write it out here.

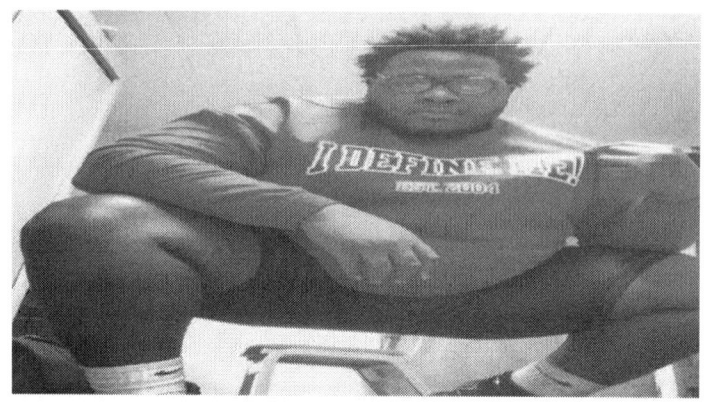

A Walk in my shoes (the short version)

Dear Lil Brotha,
I wanted to share a few chapters out of my life. No way for me to paint the picture, by giving you the short version. So, get comfortable as I break it down. It's my truth, judge me not. I may fall, but I keep getting back up. No man can walk in my shoes…

Allow me to introduce myself, My name is Justin Wyms. Currently, I am in the summer of my sophomore year of college and I have six brothers and one sister (Two of them aren't my brother but they grew up with me, so I consider them a part of my family). We have different mothers, but we never called one another "step brothers" because my dad didn't want that. Therefore, they are all my siblings. That's how we do it from where I'm from.

Presently, I attend school in San Antonio, Texas. I have a few hobbies. I like to draw, read short stories, make people laugh, buy shoes, listen to ALL music, volunteer (when I can of course), write, and lift weights. I started lifting in the 6th grade with a good man who I call my uncle till this day and a teammate who I consider my cousin. Bonding with my village is what makes a brotherhood strong.

My FUTURE goal is to be one of the World's Strongest Men. I watched these competitions as a child and it was always in the back of mind even though I played football for most of my life. The man who I've become today is someone who has been through a lot in life. I have grown out of the "please others, then myself" phase and this happened in high school. I am happy, tough, humble, and have a good relationship with my God.

Yet, I am still afraid to be great. Let me explain. My journey that leads to the person I am now began at the age of 12. I felt like I became an adult at an early age. I was making sacrifices for my family and not for myself. My brother and I would have to walk home from school and be at the house by ourselves and wait for our mother to come home from working hours, but this change was different. It was scary. Before this life-changing moment, my mother was making good money working at a nursing home. On the wealthier side of St. Louis. We didn't have the latest car, but we were up to date with the year.

My brothers always met at our house because we had the bigger house to hold all of us in. My mother always splurged on all of us for our birthdays, holidays, and special sports events like the Super Bowl. I remember the long receipts from Walmart and Toys-R-Us. They would excite me because everyone was happy, and everybody got each item they put on their list.

As time goes on, I grew older along with my other brothers, but we were separated in different parts of the same city. Yet, we only saw each other during the holidays. This particular season my mother had been struggling with some of the bills; but she made an arrangement with the landlord on how should could make payments for rent and things along that accord. Now, I won't say that we always had the money to pay all our bills on time, because my mom made payment arrangements with the utility companies, so they wouldn't shut off the services all at once.

We have had our water, electricity, and gas turned off multiple times, but my mother being the strong person she was and still is made some kind of way to get the money and get the bills paid. This particular day, my mother had taken the payment to the landlord's home and dropped the check in their mailbox which fell to the floor when placed on the inside

My mother got a call from the wife of the landlord and she was demanding the payment for the month and my mother kept trying to explain to her that she had took the check to their house, but she repeatedly said she couldn't find it in the mail received that day.

This brought a lot of stress on my entire immediate family, which included my fourteen-year-old brother and myself as I was twelve at the time. As I stated before, this was a life changing moment in our lives. As time elapsed throughout the day, She visited our home with an apology; stating that she'd found the check, but we had to leave the house because we were already behind in payments, but the landlord had; had enough of the tardiness of our payments.

I remember the day very vividly. It was an average Spring afternoon in St. Louis. My brothers and I were wrestling outside and having a great time with each other for hours this day. The mood was carried from inside when my mother was told to when I waved goodbye to Mrs. Monroe. I knew that she wasn't just stopping by because she had never done so.

When my brothers left to go home, my mother sat my older brother and I down and told us the news. I was always an emotional person as a child and still am today. When she told us this, it didn't dawn on me because I thought the process was simple; we move out and get another house. It wasn't as simple as I imagined though.

For those who don't know, when you are evicted from a home, you are granted, by law, 30 days to find a new place to stay or do whatever you need to for those days granted. I remember packing up my clothes and other miscellaneous items and it finally hitting me. I stopped packing, balled my fists up and let the waterfall of tears runs down my face. I will never forget this pain that the landlord brought onto my family and me.

The next thing I know is my mother approaching me and comforting me.

I hated to see her cry because that would've made me to cry. I remember asking her, "Why would they do this?" She had no answers for me and it made me even more angry. I remember throwing away a lot of my favorite toys and other things that meant a lot to me because I wasn't caring for anything at that moment. She asked me why I was throwing them away and I just replied, "I don't know."

We had become homeless after this incident and had to move in with our grandma who knew we were being evicted before we did but didn't tell us because she thought it would be better if we heard It from our own mother.

You see, my family was split up at this time. My older brother attended a trade school in the county while my mother and I moved in with my grandma and her husband. She made it as hospitable as she could but was mean sometimes.
I'm not sure it was intentional; it was just her way of dealing with life. We had to deal with it because literally; we had no other place to go. We stayed there for 1 year and were told to move out because her husband said so I remember my grandma crying because we left a few days before she said we had to leave. I am not sure what her feeling was, but she was very hurt by the looks of her face.

We then moved to my mother's friend's home along with her three children and inconsistent boyfriends she had at the time. We had to move all our things into her basement that was finished, but still wasn't what we wanted.

We wanted our own privacy, just like they had theirs before we came in. Immediately, I felt that we were unwanted, intruding, but she said she didn't mind at all. There were many days where our "privacy" was invaded and there was nothing we could've done about it.

Her friend was very deceiving and made it her business to make things better to accommodate to her living and not ours. I understood early during our time of living there that we'd always have that grey area where neither family wanted to be bothered with each other.

My family was reunited this time and that's all I desired. My brother still attended his trade school, though. I was happy that we kept our educations up to par even though we were going through what we were. I was in middle school during this time.

I also was playing football. This was my way out of the situation at home. I didn't want to leave my family there every night for practice, but I prayed that they were safe when I left. I don't know why I was praying, but it seemed like the right thing to do at the time.

Prayer goes a very long way and has and still does for my family and me. It is powerful. We were raised in the church and my mom made it her business to take us to church and keep that faith in our hearts.

Someone can take all your materialistic things like your money, car, phone, or clothes, but they can't take your will power and your faith. I learned a lot during this downtime, as I call it. Prayer is one of those tools to place in your playbook. I didn't know this then, but I do now.

Everyone is willing to help you to a certain point in your life. Many men, coaches, teacher, mentors and friends have been a blessing to me. That's why when you are being helped, you should take advantage of the opportunity, so you don't have to come back into that situation.

By this time, I was in high school at a wonderful private high school called Chaminade College Preparatory School for boys. I was blessed to live on campus and play football there as well. My mother and brother still lived at the house. After a year, we were told to my mother's friend was being evicted. This meant they were going to go wherever they were and we were on our own to find our own place to stay. My mother had been contacting people for long hours of the day asking if we could stay with them.

Finally, we called a family friend of ours as a last resort. This was a family that we were very grateful for. They made a way for my family to stay in a hotel for a few days with groceries and other things we needed. I was very worried that they would be on the streets or somewhere; while I was living in what seemed like luxury to me. I never talked about my issues at home, but I knew that it was affecting my academics and athletics.

It was a relief when I heard they were somewhere safe. Once again when we left, there was shock on the faces of the homeowner. There was no reason to look shocked at all. We were told we had to leave, so we did just that. Time goes on and we must leave the hotel and live with family again long enough for my mother to get some money saved so we could make a down payment. We just wanted to be in something we could call our own.

We didn't have our own place of living until my sophomore year of high school. We didn't have much to move in with, but it was a place to call our own. I had somewhere to come home to for the holidays and somewhere to enjoy my family in private. My mother and brother still found a way to get to every football game I had. I was so excited to see their faces after the games whether we won or lost. I could put more focus into football and academics when I knew they were in a safe place. I cared about their smiles and hugs after each game. That's who I would do anything for. My family.

This brings us back to the present, where I am now in life. We are all working to help each other and keep this roof above our heads. It will get better and we know it will because of the faith we have in God and in each other. We still struggle, but everybody struggles in their own way. We fall, but we get back up, we recover. We never give up!

Long story short. Never allow life to weigh you down! I'm a fighter, no one can ever walk in my shoes, but my hope is that you can learn a few lessons from my journey! God has a plan for us all! We just gotta **Keep** walking, **Keep** fighting and **Keep** getting back up. Know who defines you! I define ME!

Your BrothaKeeper, **Men**Tor
Justin Wyms

Mental Note:

Define what "walking in your own shoes" means to you? Remember NO one can write your story but you! No matter how long or short. It's your story to share so write it out. Start here. Your story starts with you!

The Brush

The brush has so many definitions, No.1 it is all about hygiene, clean hair, fresh cut and the 360 waves. Not sure how you sport your waves, but it is important to feel good about yourself inside and out. If you ever wanted waves, the kind that swim you must understand it is a true process. Like most things in life, it takes time. Just like setting goals and dreams, the journey in life you have to have faith that you are going to reach your goals. Well, when you are in the process of brushing your hair

trying to get *waves* when there is nothing there, you gotta believe they are coming!
You become usta brushing day in and day out and still no results but you don't give up.
Some do and will, this is all about the process. Eventually, because you have faith in the process it allows you to continue further down the road, whereas; some people give up, the bumps come, and either they just cut it all off and start over or just allow it to grow out.

Tell me why does the human brain process, sometimes midway through the process as you get closer to your goal or as you get to a finish line you slow down and sometimes you even give up versus going faster or pushing through? Just know if you stop you will never see the natural results and progression.

So three things:
1. Never give up on the process.
2. When you reach your goal, and you will! Stay focused and be consistent, and in a small matter of time all your hard work will be worth the wait. Until then…
3. Keep brushing and ride the waves.

10 STEPS TO 360 WAVES (the process)

1. Get a short haircut and edge up. Coarse hair can wave at shorter lengths than straight or medium hair. Don't let the barber cut your hair too low. Tell him you still want it thick—you shouldn't be able to see your scalp.
2. Brush your hair for 1-2 minutes with a wave-brush (get a hard, medium, or soft brush depending on your hair texture.)
3. Add a good moisturizer to your hair. (Coconut oil) Avoid washing your hair too much. Some wash once a week, or every other week even. Just rinse your hair instead.
4. Put a washcloth in running hot water, squeeze some water from the rag, and then place hot washcloth on top of your hair and wipe down. You can also wet a washcloth or towel and heat it up in the microwave to get it hot enough.
5. Repeat hot water process for the sides and back of hair

6. You can also brush your hair right after shampooing and conditioning in the shower. This is when your hair is softest. Just add a moisturizer and skip the hot towel part.

7. Find the point on your head where a cowlick forms, and brush out from that point to the front, sides, and back, not missing any part of your head.

8. Brush for at least 20 strokes to every side of your head, or about 15 - 30 minutes.

9. Place a wave cap or du-rag onto your head afterwards for 30 minutes, and brush again after you take it off. Make sure you sleep with the du-rag on to keep your waves from getting messed up.

10. It may take up to 6 weeks for waves to appear, so try to repeat this process daily to train your hair to form deep 360 waves. If your waves start going away, you're not brushing enough. The waves are a result of you training your hair to lay down on your head. It takes practice and patience! **Just like Life**

Mental Note:

Define what "The Brush" means to you? What habits, and hygiene tips do you routinely do to make sure that you take care of yourself every day. (Shower, Deodorant, Shampoo hair, Etc) List them below.

The Main EVENT

Dear Son,

As a man born in a totally different generation, born in the 60's, I could write my own book but I choose not too. I would like to share some defining moments or bullet points in my life that I feel you could learn from. We all can learn from one another, If you don't believe me well keep living…Life is all about embracing changes and these events not only changed me but made me the man I am today. So allow me to explore defining events in my life that changed me:

The first event was being born to two parents, not one, that chose to commit themselves to making sure that all of my needs were met. *IF you have parents that are committed to you, be thankful, thank them. When boxing with the hardships of life, it is nothing like having a solid foundation to land on.*

- Learn the definition of love, the importance of family and why it should be respected. *IF you're not close to your family, respect your friends and demand it back. Friends may be sometimes end up being closer than your blood family.*

- I was well schooled on racism by my parents and strong black leaders we had in the 60's. They all stressed the importance of building a strong foundation through education and how it was going to affect my life growing up in America as a young black man. *IF you have the opportunity to attend school, go! Know racism exist so you must be equipped to deal with school of life as well!*

- *No matter how diverse the world may be, racism, hate and bigotry will exist so stay woke! Remember, no can take away your education. You hold the key!*

- The second event was meeting the first love of my life and learning that there was another kind of love, different from family love that I had a lot to learn about. *IF and when you fall in love and you will know that 1st loves may not last forever but friends do so cherish the memories. So always be a gentleman, No matter your age, girls deserve respect, treat her like a lady from the beginning to the end.*

- The third event happened when I was 16 years of age. My first love and I were blessed with a beautiful baby girl. This event changed my life forever and required me to become a man. *IF this happens, I would not recommend it, but know that there are too many things that you think you know but find yourself learning as you go. BE accountable for your actions. Remember, Step up and be a man.*

- The first priority in your life is to educate yourself which will give you the tools you need to support yourself. Going to college for 4 years is the best way but it is not for everyone so let's not forget about the 2- year trade schools. Whatever it takes make sure you get educated so that you can take care of you and your family should one come along. *IF, obstacles arise and they will just remember you can take an education anywhere, it will stay with you for a lifetime and it is something no one can ever take away from you.*

- No matter what your goals in life are never give up. If you don't succeed at first keep trying. Success is achieved through hard work and remember; you can be whatever you want to be. *IF, you choose not to try, it's all on you.* \

- Don't be afraid to say I am sorry, your word is everything, *if you have made a mistake ,apologize it means a lot.*

- Finally, GOD who has always been there for me will be there for you. He gives second chances to those who ask for them so develop a strong relationship with him. *IF, you find yourself struggling know God defines all moments so reading this book was not by chance, God defined this moment for you as well! Find God, and you will find yourself!*

Define your Moment,
A.L. Berry, Dad, Grandfather, Engineer

Mental Note:

Define what "Main Event" or events in your life have happened that you will never forget? How does it make you feel? Share your story or Interview an elder in your life and ask them to share main events in their lives and take mental notes.

The Men Tour
(The "Talk" with my Teenage Black Son)

Not much has changed since '72
A time when I thought, or maybe I knew
That the shared candy necklaces and fire hydrant sprays
On the streets where I lived
…with the friends that I played

This was my hood, my set, my block
A place that seem safe, but truly, it was not
So I ask that you heed
The words, slurs, verbs and pronouns
…of this profound, message that
Resonates and capitulates
To an old man's epithet

Because it's YOU that I fear, when you walk out that door,
Who will cease to exist, and I cannot ignore
The talk among talks…not the birds and the bees
It's how you must act…
will you listen please?

Yes…this IS your hood, your set, your block
I'm just trying to tell you how…to not get yourself shot
It's more than two hands high, plain view sight
Both hands on a steering wheel
It's a…no Son don't…please cooperate
To keep you safe, parental plea and appeal

Far from an Uncle Tom stigma…
You're an enigma to a man with a badge,
gun and different skin tone
Don't even think about reaching for that cell phone
With hope it's…me you can call
No Son…stay focused

Resist the urge to lash out and retaliate
Stay strong…stand tall…even when they emasculate
Now that it's 18, not as in year, but more so…your age
Remember we fight not with our fist…and must harness
our inner rage

You see…not much has changed since '72
Except it's me on this end of the conversation…staring at
you. I now see clearly what my parents saw in me
In my hood, my set, on my city streets

And as your journey takes to…
foreign hoods, desolate streets, and dark corridors
Remember you control your mind…so the decision is
always yours
You with your Black face, dark skin, and pride that you
store
Remember this talk…my Son…
a talk from your mentor.

By
Eric Jerome Custard, Mentor/Father/Author
Government Civilian, Dept. of the Army

Mental Note:

Define what "The Talk" means to you? What have you learned from your Dad/Coach or Mentor that you will never forget?

The Game

Hey Bro,
I wanted to talk little bit about girls and how they can impact our lives. I went to an all-boys school from 7th-12th grade. So girls have always been the highlight of my day; especially after being around boys all the time, after practice, after homework, after chores, etc.

I didn't have much time, so my game had to be on point. I must admit I do have the confidence that most girls like and taking care of myself, staying clean, fresh cut, nice clothes and shoes was a must. Seriously, if you have confidence in yourself your winning half the game.

The rest of the game is to know that flat out, girls are not a game, girls are girls that must be respected, cherished and protected.

Seriously, I want to give you 10 pointers that you can take as advice, as well as you adding to the list...

1. Try to be friends, a girl best friend can be better than a girlfriend because you also have someone to bounce girl stuff off of, a hangout partner to kickback, go to movies, dances, concerts, etc.

2. Respect, Respect, Respect a girls' NO, she should know her worth, but if she doesn't, know that all girls deserve it, regardless of what they think of themselves. Girls love compliments but if ain't true don't say it. (Just keepin it real)

3. Don't share their secrets, some girls can be messy, and some bros talk too much, so be a keeper to their secrets.

4. Practice being a Gentlemen, open doors, censor your negative words and if you can pay for the date, do it! A man should NEVER let a girl pay for anything!

5. BE responsible. Don't depend on anyone else to cover you, you don't ever want to be in situations that can change your life because you were irresponsible.

6. Don't ever say that L-O-V-E word if you don't mean it! (repeat this 3 times) girls take that word very seriously and so should you

7. Remember break ups are hard, but not harder than a broken heart, don't cheat, just ended it. You will feel better later and so will she.

8. Know just because a girl is pretty on the outside don't mean she is pretty on the inside.

9. Know that girls have friends and they watch everything you do, don't sweat them just do you!

10. Finally, you really do have time, so take your time. Good girls are worth the wait! Good girls know their worth and so should you!

Your **MEN**tor,

Nate P. McGhee

*Men*tal *Note:*
Define what "The Game " means to you?
Add to the list?

TTG (Trained To Go)

Nephew,

I know you may be wondering what life has in store for you, we all do, but what is most important is how you walk through life. Your character, determination and will power to survive. What I do know is that your word means everything! What we say back in the day is your word is bond! SO take my advice, I live by it! I do as I say I will, you should do the same throughout life. I promise you'll earn respect from people you never met! This is all a part of surviving and winning the game!

Let's take a walk down memory lane… I'm the youngest of 6 kids, 5 half and one by the same Mother and Father. My parents where both go getters, my Mom somehow got hired as a secretary for a major aerospace company called McDonald Douglas (now Boeing) at a time when we were still considered less than formidable. She not only completed the tasks at hand daily but eventually evolved to supervise clerical duties for over 70 executives.

My Father worked for Rexall (an industrial company) for years, during that time he was diagnosed with kidney failure and had to have a transplant. My Aunt was a match and she so thankfully granted him one of hers. Then at the age of 40 he went back to school and received his accreditation for electrical engineering. My Mom then got him hired on as a tech installing electronics and missiles for McDonald Douglas.

We skip over to a gentleman I loved dearly...my 1st cousin, the son of my Aunt whom gave my father her kidney. My cousin and I both grew up in the city, we both endured gangs, drugs, murder and everything thing else ugly about inner city self -distraction you can imagine.

Fast forward a bit to his now gang life, he is at the wrong place at the wrong time and kills a man. He's convicted and received two life sentences, one w/o the possibility of parole. That means you will never come home!

Around this time my parents had recently divorced, Pop moved to ATL with his new wife and my Mother was dying from leukemia.

I'm only 15 years old at that time, and my Pop has already been gone for about 4 yrs. I see what's happening around me and I take a turn for the worst. I'm a product of my environment, as we all are.

I'll skip past all the excitement in my life for the next decade and a half. I'm now in my early 30's and I've been able to overcome some major obstacles, some self- inflicted and some not.

At this point after $10's of thousands spent on my cousins' legal fees, his sentence without parole is overturned. Wow, he didn't let the system break him.

My father does so well with the kidney he was giving it has last almost twice as long as a normal transplant and is allowed to obtain a second kidney which is something that really never happens, seriously like never. He was over 60 at this point, they normally would call it a wrap and give a kidney to a younger person.

To sum all this up, I give you this. A mother working her fingers to the bone to provide for her family whether she had a man to help or not. A man determined to live his life to the fullest and not take it for granted after almost dying. As well as another man not letting his circumstances over take his life and using them to better himself and others while on his journey.

These are my examples of self-preservation and believing in a better day. I learned from others to keep pushing, to learn how to play the game. There's no way I could give up on my family, family is all we got and achieving the highest goals I can possibly imagine. Will always keep me pushing to make my dreams a reality.

Listen, I come from one of the worst areas in the city but I didn't let it define me. I chose to take the positive and use it as the anchor in my life! In the words of the next generation, I'm TTG... trained to go. Try me! Stay on the boat, Keep sailing.

Good luck and don't let a present ugly determine your bright future! Make it Beautiful.

Holla!!!
Mike Frazier, Husband, Father, Entrepreneur, Owner of Frazier Automotive

*Men*tal *Note:*

Define What Trained to Go (TTG) means to you? What lessons have you learned? What will you take away? Create a list and begin to Dominate your life!

*

*

*

*

*

Define your Dreams!

Lil Bro,
My name is Officer Aloni Benson borned and raised in one of poorest cities in Missouri called Berkeley, neighbors to the now well known city Ferguson known for killing Mike Brown.

I was raised in a community full of demons, crime, drugs and alcohol. My brother and I was raised by my grandmother a strong black woman from down south who refuse to see us fail! She loved us, gave us her all and believed in our dreams. I know she prayed for our protection daily.

I want to talk to you about dreams because your dreams will allow you to see past your present situation. Like I said I had several real life nightmares, my mom and dad dealt with their demons, too many to name and I had to learn to fight mine.

Let me tell you, I was a fighter, at times held on to my feelings and when I blew, it was a storm so I had to learn to control my anger in a positive way.

My fight began with wrestling in High School! It gave me a fighting chance. School was cool but wrestling helped me get out my anger and be discipline and follow rules at the same time. My grandmother made us follow rules as well! Like
I said she was no joke.

3 life lessons you gotta know …

No. 1 there will be rules in life. You may not want to follow them, but if not be prepared for the consequences. The streets don't care about you! So think smart and stay on your feet. Don't allow the streets lead you! Break the cycle!

I knew I wanted to get out the hood, go to college and be somebody! I always wanted to be a police officer even though our community had lost respect for officers. I must admit I too, grew up fearing for my life when driving black or walking with my black and brown brothers just to hang out and having to break out running due to gunshots.
Yup, our communities has its issues no doubt.

What I did know was I wanted to make it out and so should you. I wanted to be a positive solution.

No. 2 Get your Education, you gotta have goals. In order to make it out I had to go to college so I did, better than a jail cell. A dorm, with friends, three meals, parties and girls! College life was the life! As a matter of fact it's where I met my wife!
Most important it's where I defined my life! I never thought a kid from Berkeley would graduate from HS, College, become a Police Officer in the County I grew up in. I made sure to get my bachelor degree and a masters. Don't just go to college, finish! My grandmother has passed on but she knew she didn't have to worry about me! I'm good! Life is challenging but a life lesson indeed.

No. 3 Leave a Legacy! And start loving challenges because that's how we overcome obstacles. I now live for my 1st born son, showing him what having a father in his life looks like, a strong black man trying to get it right. I just want to say never give up on your dreams, set your goals and go for them! I'm not a perfect man but I'm a man that strives for perfection

Remember, your BrothaKeeper is out here pushing for you! We all we got, so go make it happen! Be the Keeper of your dreams. Dominate to the fullest!

Peace in the Streets,
Officer Loni B., Father, BrothaKeeperSTL Mentor

Mental Note:

Define what "Defining your dreams and goals" means to you? What do you dream to do to Dominate Life?

Nate's PLAYBOOK Favorite Sayings

"Keep Livin" Is often stated to a younger person by an elder, to stress the importance of living and learning and realizing that you don't have all the answers. What I realize is that wisdom isn't gained overnight, we must learn to listen. Listen and Learn. As the saying goes,
We might even learn something.

"Time will tell" when applying this you can USE THIS FOR EVERYDAY LIFE. Now you may ask what does that mean... It can mean several things from working your way up as a freshman from being on Junior Varsity to starting on Varsity no matter the steps time will tell.

When I was playing football my earlier years before I continued my journey on to college, I felt that I should be starting on the field just as everyone else does. The difference though is nobody cares! You can scream and shout all you want or complain. One thing I had to learn was that the time will tell. I did not let that discourage me from the grind nor stop my dream. I continued to work day in day out and over the years the time had paid off and even when I thought my work was going unnoticed; I was WRONG!

By my junior year I was starting during playoffs when it was crucial and held my position clean through the playoffs heading into state.

The amazing thing about time is that it doesn't just apply to football it applies to life as well. My dad says **"You live and you learn!"** Have you ever met someone or began a relationship with a female and had a feeling but just did not know about the person weather it's going to end good or bad? It is only one way to figure that out and that is through time. Patience is a virtue something everyone must practice. I'm still learning and I promise you as the saying goes, time will tell. Just wait and see.

"Everybody will not go where you grow" This quote is very meaningful, because it allows us to reflect on our daily experiences. There will be a time and place in all our lives when we will accomplish things or go places where we may leave friends, love ones, and even yourself. Now you may ask what do you mean even to yourself?

My challenge was going off to college, not everyone goes to college, in addition to playing a sport on the collegiate level, in my case it was football. Some of my high school friends may have chosen college but their sport career was over. When going off to college, you will establish a new beginning in life; you will have supporters but not everyone can hold your hand through YOUR journey. You may have experiences requiring you to hold your own hand and redefine who you are, you may lose a sense of who you are, or feel you have changed. Just say true to self!

You should change, no one goes off to college and stays the same, the journey is about change. So get ready! Get ready to change, get use to saying goodbye to some and hello to someone new. Most important get ready to grow, get ready to learn more about being all you need to be for you.

They say **"Birds of a Feather flock together,"** do you agree? It is very important to choose who you hang around because birds of a feather flock together. If you can't look around at your friends and know they are like brothers, fall back. You should push each other forward or if not hit the reset button because you can only go as far as the people around you. You shouldn't always be the smartest in the bunch! You should all be leaders. You can't remain positive in a sea of negativity, eventually you will down. Sometimes it's much easier to let go than pick everyone up who's behind remember that!

Finally, **"Time waits for no one"**…I take this to mean three things.

1. Opportunity comes to those who are ready, so always be ready. Be ready to try, try, and try again.

2. Be Optimistic, know that your time will come, so have a plan of what you will do with it when your number is called.

3. Why wait for the time to come, the clock will never stop ticking so beat the clock and get their early!

Nate's Playbook Favorite Quotes

"Knowledge is Power." Francis Bacon

"Your word is Bond." Melvyn Douglas

"If you surround yourself around your dreams/goals soon it will become your reality."- Nate McGhee

"The spirit of the individual is determined by his dominating thought habits." Bruce Lee

"You will never be greater than the thoughts that dominate your mind."- Johann Wolfgang Von Goethe

"Instead of proving others wrong, prove yourself right."-Anonymous

Change will not come if we wait for some other person or some other time. We are the ones we've been waiting for. We are the change we seek." – President, Barack Obama

It's lack of faith that makes people afraid of meeting challenges, and I believed in myself."- Muhammad Ali

"I have discovered in life that there are ways of getting almost anywhere you want to go, if you really want to go." Langston Hughes

"Success is to be measured not so much by the position that one has reached in life as by the obstacles which he has overcome while trying to succeed" Booker T. Washington

"When you can do the common things in life in an uncommon way, you will command the attention of the world." George Washington Carver

"There is no better adversity. Every defeat, every heartbreak, every loss, contains its own seed, its own lesson on how to improve your performance next time" Malcolm X

*Men*tal *Note:*
What are your favorite quotes?

What does Dominate mean to you?

(DO, mi, NATE) for me, means I must do me, live my best life; knowing I am my biggest competition. I must **D**efine my journey. **O**vercoming obstacles, **making** it happen with **I**ntellect and a positive mindset. **N**ever giving up. Knowing who I belong too. Being an **A**sset. **T**aking risk. Being **E**mpowered to win!

In closing, I have many friends, team players and young men that I call my brothers and we all agree sports has taught us a million life-lessons, but I will leave you with this! Every obstacle can be a struggle, but it is up to you to define how you will DOMINATE it.

You always have a choice, so choose. Life is too short to just exist, so live your life to the fullest. Be responsible, be humble, be ready and know in order to win you must stay in the game! It's not always about keeping score, who wins or loses but the lessons you learn that allow you to keep living! This book is my example trying to do just that. Make it happen! Dominate the Norm. Dominate Life!

Your MENtor,

Nate P. McGhee

"TO be a MAN- "EstoVir"

Chaminade College Preparatory Graduate 2017

Boys to MENTOR

"Life is about being a versatile athlete and training in all realms of life."-Ray Lewis

"Begin with the end in mind and die empty."- Aeneas Williams

"My journey is just beginning...to be continued!"~

Student/Athlete, Nathaniel P. McGhee

Special ShoutOuts

GOD
My Mother & Father the McGhee's
My Sisters Khalia Benson & Bria McGhee
Brother Aloni Benson
Patrice Dulaney
Grandma Corinne & Grandpa Odell
My Grandfather Barcland McGhee
MahMah, Margo Hamilton
Grandpa-Arthur Berry
Joy Edwards
Miles Williams
Justin Wyms
Mike Frazier
Aeneas Williams
Cory Sauls
Art Green
Dietrich Smith (Groovy)
Joyce Anderson
Rev. Traci Blackmon
C. Jerome Thompson
Thomas Watkins
Ron Kirk
Mike Baker
Keith Jones
To those who I forgot, please charge it to my mind and not my heart!

For Booking Info: Products and more please visit

IG: DominateSTL
www.dominateSTL.com

Made in the USA
Columbia, SC
15 May 2019